WE COULDN'T PROVIDE FISH THUMBS

Also published by Macmillan

ONE OF YOUR LEGS IS BOTH THE SAME
Poems by Adrian Henri, Terry Jones,
Michael Rosen, Colin McNaughton
and Kit Wright

ANOTHER DAY ON YOUR FOOT AND
I WOULD HAVE DIED
Poems by John Agard, Wendy Cope,
Roger McGough, Adrian Mitchell
and Brian Patten

We Couldn't Provide Fish Thumbs

Poems by
James Berry
Grace Nichols
Judith Nicholls
Vernon Scannell
Matthew Sweeney

Illustrated by Colin McNaughton

MACMILLAN CHILDREN'S BOOKS

First published 1997 by Macmillan Children's Books

This edition published 1998 by Macmillan Children's Books
a division of Macmillan Publishers Ltd
25 Eccleston Place London SW1W 9NF
and Basingstoke

Associated companies throughout the world

ISBN 0 330 35236 9

A CIP catalogue record for this book is available from the British Library.

Typeset by Macmillan Children's Books
Printed and bound in Great Britain by Mackays of Chatham PLC, Kent

Contents

Special Today

We can recommend our soups
        And offer thick or thin.
One is known as 'Packet',
        The other known as 'Tin'.

The flying fish makes a very fine dish;
        As good as plaice or skate
When sizzled in fat; but be certain that
        You tether it to your plate.

Now this hot dog makes an excellent snack;
        Our sausages are best pork.
If you can't get it down, please don't send it back,
        Take it for a nice brisk walk.

Are you tempted by our fried fish fingers?
        The last customer to succumb
Was hard to please; he demanded
        Why we couldn't provide a fish thumb.

Bubble and squeak is splendid stuff,
    And Chef takes endless trouble.
But if you feel you'd like a change
    Then try our squeak and bubble.

If you choose our historical steak
    You'll chew and chew and chew
And know what Joan of Arc,
    When tied to one, went through.

You may have tried most kinds of pie
    But have you ever dared
To munch a circular portion of
    Crusty πr^2?

Try our cabinet pudding
    Or a slice of home-made cake;
We serve with each, quite free of charge,
    A pill for your belly ache.

Vernon

Mosquito

I am
go-as-you-please,
easy houseguest;
I ask no fuss.
My one request,
a little space
to spread my wing.
No lace-edged tablecloth
or grand settee,
no silver dish
or cutlery . . .
Just you
and me.

I am
a simple pet.
I need no lead,
no need for kennel, collar,
cage or vet.
My gentle buzz
is far more sweet
than wasp's or bee's.
I'd never tease or groan,
or eat you out of house and home . . .
A little bite
is quite enough.

So why,
please tell me why . . . ?

Lines

I must never daydream in schooltime.
I just love a daydream in Mayshine.
I must ever greydream in timeschool.
Why must others paydream in schoolway?
Just over highschool dismay lay.
Thrust over skydreams in cryschool.
Cry dust over drydreams in screamtime.
Dreamschool thirst first in dismayday.
Why lie for greyday in crimedream?
My time for dreamday is soontime.
In soontime must I daydream ever.
Never must I say dream in strifetime.
Cry dust over daydreams of lifetimes.
I must never daydream in schooltime.
In time I must daydream never.

Ar-A-Rat

I know a rat on Ararat,
He isn't thin, he isn't fat
Never been chased by any cat
Not that rat on Ararat.
He's sitting high on a mountain breeze,
Never tasted any cheese,
Never chewed up any old hat,
Not that rat on Ararat.
He just sits alone on a mountain breeze,
Wonders why the trees are green,
Wonders why the ground is flat,
O that rat on Ararat.
His eyes like saucers, glow in the dark –
The last to slip from Noah's ark.

Grace

Ritual Sun Dance

O sun O sun –
noon eye of noon time breath
makes blooms come,
unfolds big trees from seeds,
stirs crusts into leaves,
dresses cold shapes *warm warm* –
excite the little grown
to be fully grown.

>   Hey-hey! Hey-hey!
>   Sun gone down. Gone down underground.
>   Come dance, come dance!
>   Don't mind who father is.
>   Don't mind who mother is.
>   Come dance and see the sun come back!

O sun O sun –
kisser who tickles crusts,
who swells yams in the ground,
fattens up droopy reeds
like apples and plums
like bananas and mangoes
like sharp spices sharper –
touch everywhere.

>   Hey-hey! Hey-hey!
>   Sun gone down. Gone down underground.
>   Come dance, come dance!
>   Don't mind no child, no herd.
>   Don't mind your sound of words.
>   Come dance and see the sun come back!

O sun O sun –
flood-flame of air,
making pods pop
making seeds drop,
grass growing to strong rum,
oranges getting brighter,
grapes getting sweeter –
drape fields, drape fields.
> Hey-hey! Hey-hey!
> Sun gone down. Gone down underground.
> Come dance, come dance!
> Don't mind what roof house is.
> Don't mind what kind dress is.
> Come dance and see the sun come back!

O sun O sun –
mighty dazzler
who moves the zero hour
moves the zero hour –
make nuts brown,
brushless,
noiseless.
> Hey-hey! Hey-hey!
> Sun gone down. Gone down underground.
> Come dance, come dance!
> Don't mind what track leads you.
> Don't mind what wheels bring you.
> Come dance and see the sun come back!

James

My Dog

My dog belongs to no known breed,
A bit of this and that.
His head looks like a small haystack.
He's lazy, smelly, fat.

If I say, 'Sit' he walks away.
When I throw a stick or ball
He flops down in the grass as if
He had no legs at all,

And looks at me with eyes that say,
'You threw the thing, not me.
You want it back, then get it back.
Fair's fair you must agree.'

He is a thief. Last week but one
He stole the Sunday Roast.
And showed no guilt at all as we
Sat down to beans on toast.

The only time I saw him run –
And he went like a flash –
Was when a mugger in the park
Tried to steal my cash.

My loyal brave companion flew
Like a missile to the gate
And didn't stop till safely home.
He left me to my fate.

And would I swap him for a dog
Obedient, clean and good,
An honest, faithful, lively chap?
Oh boy, I would! I would!

Vernon

In the Desert

Wrapped in my camelhair rug
I'm camouflaged
out here in the desert.
My feet make no sound on the sand.
The sky is crawling with stars.

I shout, and it echoes
all the way to the sea.
No answering cry comes back to me.
I could be the last boy,
I could be up on the moon.

Nothing but flat for miles,
the occasional bone
strewn on the sand.
I take one back with me
to help bury my parachute.

I check my compass
and head due south-east.
A light wind covers my footprints.
I have no need of water.
I'll hit the oasis by dawn.

Matthew

Come on into my Tropical Garden

Come on into my tropical garden
Come on in and have a laugh in
Taste my sugar cake and my pine drink
Come on in please come on in

And yes you can stand up in my hammock
and breeze out in my trees
you can pick my hibiscus
and kiss my chimpanzees

O you can roll up in the grass
and if you pick up a flea
I'll take you down for a quick dip-wash
in the sea
believe me there's nothing better
for getting rid of a flea
than having a quick dip-wash in the sea

Come on into my tropical garden
Come on in please come on in

Grace

Stickers

I can't bear all those car rear-windows
       Plastered with daft words;
My missus drives a broomstick – that is
       Strictly for the birds.

I don't care if he *loves his Mini*,
       Has a *Dog on board*
Or if he is a *Spurs supporter*
       Or where he's been abroad.

Keep your distance – he should worry!
       Not at any price
Would I venture any closer
       To his fluffy dice.

Short vehicle. Not long, you geddit?
       What a witty spread!
A dozen stickers on his window,
       Nothing in his head!

Vernon

The Girl I did not Marry

When I was eighteen years of age
        I met a lovely girl;
She was so beautiful she made
        My thoughts and senses whirl.

Not only beautiful but kind,
        Intelligent as well;
Her smile was warm as India,
        Her voice, a silver bell.

So gentle and so sensitive,
        She was the one for me;
We loved the same great melodies
        And peace and poetry.

In spring we wandered hand in hand
        Towards a treasured scene
To which I'd never taken her,
        Small paradise of green.

We climbed a gentle slope and then
        Walked through a little wood;
And there, below, were shining fields
        Where sheep and young lambs stood

Or danced or drifted on dry seas,
    Their bleatings frail or hoarse.
'When I see those,' my darling said,
    'I always smell mint sauce.'

Vernon

Break Dance

I'm going to break dance
turn rippling glass
stretch my muscles
to the bass

Whoo!

I'm going to break/dance
I'm going to rip it
and jerk it
and take it apart

I'm going to chop it
and move it
and groove it

Ooooh I'm going to ooze it
electric boogaloo
electric boogaloo
across your floor

I'm going to break/dance
watch my ass
take the shine
off you laugh

Whoo!

I'm going to dip it and spin it
let my spine twist it
I'm going to shift it
and stride it
let my mind glide it

Then I'm going to ease it
ease it
and bring it all home
all home
                    believing in the beat
                    believing in the beat
                    of myself

Grace

Cows on the Beach

Two cows,
fed-up with grass, field, farmer,
barged through barbed wire
and found the beach.
Each mooed to each:
This is a better place to be,
a stretch of sand next to the sea,
this is the place for me.
And they stayed there all day,
strayed this way, that way,
over to rocks,
past discarded socks,
ignoring the few people they met
(it wasn't high season yet).
They dipped hooves in the sea,
got wet up to the knee,

they swallowed pebbles and sand,
found them a bit bland,
washed them down with sea-water,
decided they really ought to
rest for an hour.
Both were sure
they'd never leave here.
Imagine, they'd lived so near
and never knew!
With a swapped moo
they sank into sleep,
woke to the yellow jeep
of the farmer
revving there
feet from the incoming sea.
This is no place for cows to be,
he shouted, and slapped them
with seaweed, all the way home. Matthew

Okay, Brown Girl, Okay

for Josie, 9 years old, who wrote to me saying . . . 'boys called me
names because of my colour. I felt very upset . . . My brother and
sister are English. I wish I was, then I won't be picked on . . .
How do you like being brown?'

Josie, Josie, I am okay
being brown. I remember,
every day dusk and dawn get born
from the loving of night and light
who work together, like married.
> And they would like to say to you:
> Be at school on and on, brown Josie
> like thousands and thousands and thousands
> of children, who are brown and white
> and black and pale-lemon colour.
> All the time, brown girl Josie is okay.

Josie, Josie, I am okay
being brown. I remember,
every minute sun in the sky
and ground of the earth work together
like married.
> And they would like to say to you:
> Ride on up a going escalator
> like thousands and thousands and thousands
> of people, who are brown and white
> and black and pale-lemon colour.
> All the time, brown girl Josie is okay.

Josie, Josie, I am okay
being brown. I remember,
all the time bright-sky and brown-earth
work together, like married
making forests and food and flowers and rain.
 And they would like to say to you:
 Grow and grow brightly, brown girl.
 Write and read and play and work.
 Ride bus or train or boat or aeroplane
 like thousands and thousands and thousands
 of people, who are brown and white
 and black and pale-lemon colour.
 All the time, brown girl Josie is okay.

How you like that?

My Cousin Melda

My Cousin Melda
she don't make fun
she ain't afraid of anyone
even mosquitoes
when they bite her
she does bite them back
and say –
'Now tell me, how you like that?'

Grace

He Loves Me, He Loves Me Not . . .

(Sing to the tune of 'Bobby Shaftoe')

Peter Packer, he loves Dee,
but she chases Johnny Lea,
Johnny says that he loves me,
Poor old Peter Packer!

Peter Packer's not too clever,
Dee says she will love him never,
he says he'll love Dee for ever,
Potty Peter Packer!

Johnny Lea is chasing Dee now,
Dee has gone off Johnny Lea now,
Peter Packer's after me now,
Perfect Peter Packer!

Juanne

Naughty Nursery Rhymes

i
The strawberry cried
'I'm in a jam!
I don't know why
But here I am.'

The little tart
Said, 'So I see.
I know because
The jam's in me.'

And Tommy Tibbs,
The greedy lad,
Scoffing both
Said, 'Just too bad!'

ii

Old Mother Hubbard
Sat in the cupboard
Eating Jack's Christmas pie.
He opened the door
Gave a furious roar
And blacked Mother Hubbard's right eye.

iii

'Twinkle twinkle little star,'
Cashbags puffs his big cigar.
'Be careful what you do and say –
You'll be a big star one fine day!'

Vernon

Into the Mixer

Into the mixer he went,
  the nosy boy,
into the mess of wet cement,
  round and round
  with a glugging sound
and a boyish screamed complaint.

Out of the mixer he came,
  the concrete boy,
onto the road made of the same
  quick-setting stuff
  He looked rough
and he'd only himself to blame.

Matthew

Pass the Pasta!

Spud
is good,
rice
is nice,
but pasta
is faster!

For Forest

Forest could keep secrets
Forest could keep secrets

Forest tune in every day
to watersound and birdsound
Forest letting her hair down
to the teeming creeping of her forest-ground

But Forest don't broadcast her business
no Forest cover her business down
from sky and fast-eye sun
and when night come
and darkness wrap her like a gown
Forest is a bad dream woman

Forest dreaming about mountain
and when earth was young
Forest dreaming of the caress of gold
Forest rootsing with mysterious Eldorado

and when howler monkey
wake her up with howl
Forest just stretch and stir
to a new day of sound

but coming back to secrets
Forest could keep secrets
Forest could keep secrets

And we must keep Forest

Grace

Jam Roll in Custody

They took him to the local nick
  And put him in a cell.
I asked what charge was being brought,
  Although I knew quite well,
For I had handled similar cases
  With logic and with charm:
I specialise in G.G.H. –
  Grievous gastric harm.

My clients have included some
  Very shifty folk:
A ham burglar and shepherd spy,
  A rather half-baked bloke;
A trickster pushing jelly deals
  And lemon soles that trample;
A seafood Highlander, who set
  A rotten Scotch egg sample.

But I, with customary skill,
  Convinced the nodding judge
That Mr Bun, the plaintiff, bore
  All kinds of roll a grudge.
Jam roll was freed and we rejoiced;
  This pastry case was won.
The loser was enraged, of course;
  A very hot cross Bun.

Vernon

Retirement Poem
For teacher, Maisie Carter

Years after years
and years after years
she wakes with shoes on
and goes
hugging books, pens, folders,
off to scatter words
in the growing of girls and boys.
Will she kick her shoes off now?

Orang-utan

Watch me,
touch me,
catch-me-if-you-can!
I am
soundless,
swung-from-your-sight,
gone with the wind,
shiver of air,
trick-of-the-light.

Watch me,
touch me,
catch-me-if-you-dare!
I hide, I glide,
I stride though the air,
shatter the day-star dappled light
over forest floor.
The world's in my grasp!
I am windsong,
sky-flier,
man-of-the-woods,
the arm of the law.

Don't Cry, Caterpillar

Don't cry, Caterpillar
Caterpillar, don't cry
You'll be a butterfly – by and by.

Caterpillar, please
Don't worry 'bout a thing

'But,' said Caterpillar,
'Will I still know myself – in wings?'

Grace

The Young and Hopeful Lover

I knew that I would have to wait
      Years and years before
I carried, as my bride, Miss Hyde
      Through my own front door.

And I was quite prepared to wait
      Patiently until
I'd go away and then, one day,
      Come back all dressed to kill.

I mean I'd be in uniform –
      Para or Marine –
And I would wait outside the gate,
      Muscular and lean.

Miss Hyde would see me standing there
      As she came out of school;
She'd be wide-eyed as I would stride
      Towards her, smiling, cool.

But now I'm told she is engaged –
      And this you'd never guess –
To Mr Trench who teaches French!
      I'm shocked, I must confess.

I should have told her of my plans –
        Or so it now appears –
I think she would have understood
        And waited a few years.

Yet I've not given up all hope.
        I still dream of the day
When I shall be grown up and free
        To carry her away!

Vernon

Emergency Stop

Dad was in a chatty mood: he said
To Jake and me, 'Before you go to bed,
I'll tell you what occurred when Uncle Joe
First took his driving-test, but don't you go
And tell him what I told you; he'd go mad!
Now, years ago, when he was just a lad,
Though old enough to take his driving-test –
The first of many as you might have guessed –
Young Joe was absolutely confident.
He simply didn't know what failure meant.
So off he went to take this easy test.
All went well, at first, and he impressed
The stern examiner with his calm skill.
But notice my "at first". I mean until
The moment came when Joe must show how he
Would stop the car in some emergency.
"I shall strike the dashboard suddenly
With my rolled newspaper," the man told Joe.
"There'll be no warning: this is meant to show
An awkward incident has just occurred,
And you must stop. I will not say a word.
You understand?"

Joe nodded and said "Yes."
They'd gone perhaps a hundred yards or less:
The signal came: the paper slapped down hard.

Joe slammed down on the brakes with no regard
For passenger or anything except
His sudden stop, and his companion leapt –
Or seemed to leap – head-first and, with a crack
Struck the windscreen, yelped, and then bounced back,
Blood spurting from his nose. Joe offered him
His hankie but the man looked very grim
And said, "Just take me back at once, that's all,
And don't go any faster than a crawl!" '
Jake asked, 'What happened, did he pass or fail?'
'He failed. And so, the moral of my tale
Is don't go to extremes, and – I suppose –
Try not to break your driving-tester's nose.'

Vernon

All the Dogs

You should have seen him –
he stood in the park and whistled,
underneath an oak tree,
and all the dogs came bounding up
and sat around him,
keeping their big eyes on him,
tails going like pendulums.
And there was one cocker pup
who went and licked his hand,
and a Labrador who whimpered
till the rest joined in.
Then he whistled a second time,
high-pitched as a stoat,
over all the shouted dog names
and whistles of owners,
till a flurry of paws
brought more dogs, panting,
as if they'd come miles,
and these too found space
on the flattened grass
to stare at the boy's
unmemorable face
which all the dogs found special.

Matthew

Date-beggin Sweet Word Them

Look ow I unexpectid –
big ello unexpectid

like new package at yu door
delivad right at yu door

to mix a lickle talk
with a sweet lickle walk

in a stroll from yu door
a-know we nevva did poor

a-hear the city a-sing
wandaful worl a-galang[1]

with we eye them a smile
everywhere all the while

and we work we new strong curves
roun the bright bright discos

eatin a fruit from each stall
with shoes on or none at all –

so June-June yu goin sey yes
we step out and feel we bes?

James

[1] *a-galang – going along*

Bubblebus

My bus will be a steel bubble
called the Bubblebus
that will roll down the empty streets
of 2010 London
where no cars will have been seen
since 1999, and only long sleek trams
will glide past me
as we stop at the bubblestops
for me to strap new passengers in.
And no one will have to pay
to ride on my bubblebus,
and no exhaust fumes
will foul London's air
because we'll be sucked along
by the huge magnets
on each terminus.
Bubblebuses, bubblebuses,
roll, roll into the near future.
I'm almost ready with the design.

Matthew

Storytime

Once upon a time, children,
there lived a fearsome dragon . . .

Please, miss,
Jamie's made a dragon.
Out in the sandpit.

Lovely, Andrew.
Now this dragon
had enormous red eyes
and a swirling, whirling tale . . .

Jamie's dragon's got
yellow eyes, miss.

Lovely, Andrew.
Now this dragon was
as wide as a horse
as green as the grass
as tall as a house . . .

Jamie's would JUST fit
in our classroom, miss!

But he was a very friendly dragon . . .

Jamie's dragon ISN'T, miss.
He eats people, miss.
Especially TEACHERS,
Jamie said.

Very nice, Andrew!
Now one day, children,
this enormous dragon
rolled his red eye,
whirled his swirly green tail
and set off to find . . .

His dinner, miss!
Because he was hungry, miss!

Thank you, Andrew.
He rolled his red eye,
whirled his green tail,
and opened his wide, wide mouth
until

Baby-K Rap Rhyme

My name is Baby-K
An dis is my rhyme
Sit back folks
While I rap my mind;

Ah rocking with my homegirl,
My Mommy
Ah rocking with my homeboy,
My Daddy
My big sister, Les, an
My Granny,
Hey dere people – my posse
I'm the business
The ruler of the nursery

poop po-doop
poop-poop po-doop
poop po-doop
poop-poop po-doop

Well, ah soaking up de rhythm
Ah drinking up my tea
Ah bouncing an ah rocking
On my Mommy knee
So happy man so happy

poop po-doop
poop-poop po-doop
poop po-doop
poop-poop po-doop

Wish my rhyme wasn't hard
Wish my rhyme wasn't rough
But sometimes, people
You got to be tough

Cause dey pumping up de chickens
Dey stumping down de trees
Dey messing up de ozones
Dey messing up de seas
Baby-K say, stop dis –
please, please, please

poop po-doop
poop-poop po-doop
poop po-doop
poop-poop po-doop

Now am splashing in de bath
With my rubber duck
Who don't like dis rhyme
Kiss my baby-foot
Babies everywhere
Join a Babyhood

Cause dey hotting up de globe, man
Dey hitting down de seals
Dey killing off de ellies
for dere ivories
Baby-K say, stop dis –
please, please, please

poop po-doop
poop-poop po-doop
poop po-doop
poop-poop po-doop

Dis is my Baby-K rap
But it's kinda plea
What kinda world
Dey going to leave fuh me?
What kinda world
Dey going to leave fuh me?

Poop po-doop.

Grace

Hairy Story

My Dad forgot to shave one day
and a few small hairs appeared.
He stroked his chin then said with a grin,
'I think I'll grow a beard!'

'Give us a hug!' cried Dad next day,
but we all disappeared!
Now Dad's chin's like scratchy pins
since he started to grow that beard!

'It's coming along,' said Dad next week.
He'd really persevered,
so we all had to hug the hairy rug
that was Dad with his new beard!

'It's doing rather well!' said Dad.
He was looking really weird.
We watched him wash and comb and brush
and curl and twirl that beard.

'*Now* what do you think of it?' asked Dad,
and we all stood round and cheered;
for a small redbreast had made his nest
in the forest that was Dad's beard!

Upper-deck Driver

When riding on a city bus
I always make my way upstairs.
I must admit I make a fuss,
And I receive some frosty stares.
The reason is, I love to play
At bus-drivers. As I sit there,
And wait for us to move away,
I grip an unseen wheel and stare
Down into the busy street;
I grunt the sound as I change gear,
Growl engine-noise, and then repeat
The change of gear. I love this game;
It really is tremendous fun,
And I don't feel the slightest shame
When people stare, as they have done.
Some have been quite angry, too.
I thought that I should ask a friend
If he believed that people who
Complained were simply round the bend.
I told him that the person who
Liked to sit and make believe
That he was driving buses through
The busy traffic was not me
But a relative of mine.
'Oh,' said my friend, 'I take it he
Is very young. What? Eight or nine?

I'd say it's normal for a boy
To sit on the top deck and steer.
For him, it's just a great big toy
He'll grow out of it, don't fear.'
'Oh dear,' I thought, with some dismay,
'If my old friend knew it was me
Who drove the bus, what would he say?
For I'm not nine, but forty-three!'

Vernon

The Burglar

When the burglar went out
to burgle a house

When the burglar pulled on
his black polo-neck,
his beret, his Reeboks

When the burglar rattled
his skeleton keys,
checked he had his street-map,
said goodbye to his budgie

When the burglar shouldered
an empty bag, big enough
to take as much swag
as the burglar could carry

When the burglar waited
for the bus

When the burglar stood
at the bottom of the street
where the house he'd picked
to burgle was

When the burglar burgled
he didn't know
that another burglar
was inside *his* house

And only the budgie would see

Matthew

Who's a pretty burglar?

My Parakeet

Anyone see my parakeet, Skeet?
He's small and neat,
He's really sweet,
with his pick-pick beak,
And his turn-back feet.

Skeet, Skeet, I wouldn't tell a lie
You are the green-pearl of my eye.

Grace

Pssst!

Have you seen
Mrs Moggett's knickers
hanging on the line?

Long, not tiny ones,
pink ones, shiny ones,
baggy ones and dotty ones,
yellow-striped and spotty ones,
giant-sized roomy ones,
blown-up-like-balloon-y ones . . .
-parachute-to-Paris
or take-you-to-the-moon-y ones . . .
Have *you* seen
Mrs Moggett's knickers
swinging on the line?

(Pssst! Don't all shout,
but Monday's when they're out!)

Morning

Morning comes
    with a milk-float jiggling

Morning comes
    with a milkman whistling

Morning comes
    with empties clinking

Morning comes
    with alarm-clock ringing

Morning comes
    with toaster popping

Morning comes
    with letters dropping

Morning comes
    with kettle singing

Morning comes
    with me just listening

Morning comes to drag me out of bed
    – Boss-Woman Morning.

Grace

The Fable of Aunty Mabel

Absent-minded Auntie Mabel
Got so drunk she was unable
To crawl out from beneath the table:
Most unlike dear Auntie Mabel!

We found out later that this awful
Scene occurred because forgetful
Mabel suffered such a woeful
Lapse of memory, almost fatal.

She forgot to put the trifle
In her favourite sherry trifle:
So this is what we like to label
Mabel's sherry-trifle fable.

Vernon

Scribbled Notes Picked up by Owners, and Rewritten
because of bad grammar, bad spelling, bad writing

Letter from YOUR SPeCiAl-BiG-pUPPy-DOg.

You know I'm so big
I'll soon become a person.
You know I want to know more
of all that you know. Yet
you leave the house, so, so often.
And not one quarrel between us.
Why don't you come home ten times
a day? Come tell me the way
your boss is bad? See me sit,
listening, sad? And you know,
and I know, it's best
when you first come in.
You call my name. And O
I go starry-eyed on you,
can't stop wagging, jumping,
holding, licking your face,
saying, 'D'you know – d'you know –
you're quite, quite a dish!'
Come home – come call my name –
every time thirty minutes pass.

Letter from Your KitTeN-cAT-AlMoSt-BiG-CaT.

You tell me to clear up
the strings of wool off
the floor, just to see how
I slink out the door. But O
you're my mum. Fifty times
big to climb on. You stroke
my back from head to tail.
You tickle my furry throat,
letting my claws needle your side,
and my teeth nibble your hand
till I go quiet. I purr.
I purr like a poor boy
snoring, after gift of a dinner.
I leap into your lap only
to start everything over.

Count Your Toes!

This little piggy
spilt his milk on the floor.

This little piggy
spilt his milk on the bed.

This little piggy
sat in his milk.

This little piggy
poured his milk on his head.

And this little piggy
drank EVERYBODY'S milk . . .

so he was sick instead!

The Porcupie

I should not try, if I were you,
To eat the porcupie;
Although the crust is brown and crisp
And packed with meat, you'll die.
Those little spikes will pierce your throat,
Those quills will make you ill,
And you will find no antidote,
No medicine or pill.
So let the little porcupie
Go quietly to its lair
And satisfy your appetite
With apple, plum or pear;
So porcupies may occupy
A world made safe for porcupies
Here and everywhere.

Vernon

When My Friend Anita Runs

When my friend Anita runs
she runs straight into the headalong –
legs flashing over grass, daisies, mounds.

When my friend Anita runs
she sticks out her chest like an Olympic
champion – face all serious concentration.

And you'll never catch her looking around,
until she flies into the invisible tape
that says, she's won.

Then she turns to give me
this big grin and hug

O to be able to run like Anita
                    run like Anita,
Who runs like a cheetah.
If only, just for once, I could beat her.

Grace

Christmas Story

Once upon a time, children,
and it was a very long time ago,
there were three men . . .

What were they called, miss?

We don't know, Andrew,
what they were called,
where they came from,
where they went.
We just know that
they were shepherds . . .

What's a shepherd, miss?

A shepherd, Andrew,
is someone who looks after . . .

Please, miss . . .

Someone who looks after . . .

*My Uncle Bill had to look after me,
last night, miss!*

SHEEP, Andrew, sheep!
A shepherd cares for sheep!
Now one night,
on a ˘dark hillside . . .

I don't like it when it's dark, miss!

On this hillside . . .

Do you think they were scared, miss?

I don't think so, Andrew.
These shepherds had been there
on the hillside,
many nights before.
They talked quietly, together,
under the stars . . .

YOU said I could have a star, miss!
For my picture. You PROMISED!

Quietly together,
under the stars,
watching their sheep . . .

Why didn't they watch Batman, miss?
Were they too scared?

This was a *very* long time ago, Andrew.
There was NO Batman.
No Batman, no Muppets,
no Blue Peter, no Grange Hill,
no Blockbusters, no Ghostbusters,
NO television!
They watched their SHEEP . . .

My Dad told me to count sheep
when I didn't want to go to bed.
Sheep'll make you sleep,
he said!

I know just what he means, Andrew!
They watched their sheep . . .

WHY did they need to watch them, miss?

To keep them safe, Andrew,
just like your Mum and Dad keep you safe.
To stop them getting lost . . .

My Mum once lost me, miss!

She must have been very . . . worried, Andrew!
But she found you again, just like . . .

It was in Woolworths, miss,
at Christmas . . .

Just like a shepherd . . .

I was scared, miss,
I was REALLY scared!

Just . . .

I didn't know where she was!
But I didn't cry, miss,
really I didn't . . .

JUST like a shepherd,
rescuing his sheep with his crook . . .

My Uncle Bill's a crook, miss!
Dad says! Dad says he once . . .

THANK you, Andrew!
Perhaps we should all sing the song we know,
about these shepherds watching their sheep
on the quiet hillside.
Then, maybe,
we could choose some children
to be the shepherds
in our Christmas play . . .

Oh, PLEASE miss,
let ME be a shepherd.
If you want a crook
I could bring my Un . . .

THANK YOU, ANDREW!

Seeing Granny

Toothless, she kisses
with fleshly lips
rounded, like mouth
of a bottle, all wet.

She bruises your face
almost, with two
loving tree-root hands.

She makes you sit, fixed.
She then stuffs you
with boiled pudding and lemonade.

She watches you feed
on her food. She milks
you dry of answers
about the goat she gave you.

My Party

Come to my party on Christmas Eve
in my rented air balloon.
Well, it's really a Zeppelin,
and at midnight you've got to leave.

Why? Because it's Christmas.
How do you get up there?
Hitch a ride on a helicopter.
Do it, and don't make a fuss,

and don't be late, or the angels
won't appear in their feathers
or their spacesuit evening wear,
and the food will go to the gulls.

The food? There'll be larks' eggs
and flying fish, and roast crow.
(Horrible? How do you know?)
And specially imported moon figs.

Oh, and coke made with rain.
What about music? The stars
helped along by meteors
will cobble together a tune.

No more questions? Good.
Write it in the diary, then,
and spread the news to a friend
immediately. Is that understood?

Matthew

Jelly-Lover

Jill likes stuff that wobbles, quivers,
Trembles and gives little shivers,
Ripples, promising rich pleasure,
Glitters like Aladdin's treasure,
Green or red or orange, yellow,
Sharp and fruity, sweet and mellow.
Jill likes jelly in her belly,
She would eat it from a welly;
Loves to see it shake and shudder,
Brightly joggle, jounce and judder.
She adores its slippery motion
And could wallow in an ocean,
Not of green and foamy briny
But lime jelly, smooth and shiny.
Jill, whose best friend calls her Jilly,
Said, 'I hope I don't sound silly
If I say my dream vacation
Has to be an invitation
To an island, gold and shining,
Where I'd spend all day reclining
By a sprinkling sherbet fountain
Shaded by a jelly mountain.'

Vernon

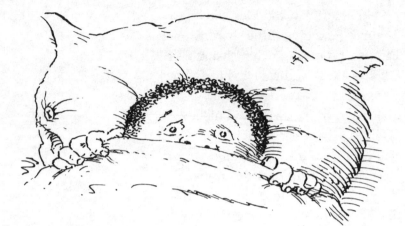

I Like to Stay Up

I like to stay up
and listen
when big people talking
jumbie¹ stories

I does feel
so tingly and excited
inside me

But when my mother say
'Girl, time for bed'

Then is when
I does feel a dread

Then is when
I does jump into me bed

Then is when
I does cover up
from me feet to me head

Then is when
I does wish I didn't listen
to no stupid jumbie story

Then is when
I does wish I did read
me book instead

Grace

[1] *jumbie – Guyanese word for 'ghost'*

Jason's Trial

Jason was a football freak;
      He really loved the game:
To be a first-class footballer
      Was his one aim.

He practised every day and played
      Again each night in dream;
When he was twelve they chose him for
      The school's first team.

He was quite brilliant. Five years passed
      And – though rarely this occurs –
It seemed his dreams might all come true:
      He was given a trial by Spurs.

He played a blinder on the day;
      The spectators cheered and roared,
And after the match he was asked to appear
      Before the Selection Board.

The Chairman said, 'I've got the reports
      From our experts who watched you play:
Your speed and ball-control were fine;
      For tackling you get an A.

'And when our striker scored his goal
      You were first to jump on his back,
And when *you* scored you punched the air
      Before you resumed the attack.

'So far, so good; but you were weak
      On the thing our lads do best;
It seems you hardly spat at all,
      So you failed the spitting-test.

'But don't despair. If you go home
      And practise every day
You still might learn to spit with style
      In the true professional way.'

Vernon

Grannie

I stayed with her when I was six then went
To live elsewhere when I was eight years old.
For ages I remembered her faint scent
Of lavender, the way she'd never scold
No matter what I'd done, and most of all
The way her smile seemed, somehow, to enfold
My whole world like a warm, protective shawl.

I knew that I was safe when she was near,
She was so tall, so wide, so large, she would
Stand mountainous between me and my fear,
Yet oh, so gentle, and she understood
Every hope and dream I ever had.
She praised me lavishly when I was good,
But never punished me when I was bad.

Years later war broke out and I became
A soldier and was wounded while in France.
Back home in hospital, still very lame,
I realised suddenly the circumstance
Had brought me close to that small town where she
Was living still. And so I seized the chance
To write and ask if she could visit me.

She came. And I still vividly recall
The shock that I received when she appeared
That dark cold day. Huge grannie was so small!
A tiny, frail, old lady. It was weird.
She hobbled through the ward to where I lay
And drew quite close and, hesitating, peered
And then she smiled: and love lit up the day.

Vernon

Listn Big Brodda Dread, Na!

My sista is younga than me.
My sista outsmart five-foot three.
My sista is own car repairer
and yu nah catch me doin judo with her.

> I sey I wohn get a complex
> I wohn get a complex.
> Then I see the muscles my sista flex.

My sista is tops at disco dance.
My sista is well into self-reliance.
My sista plays guitar and drums
and wahn see her knock back double rums.

      I sey I wohn get a complex
      I wohn get a complex.
      Then I see the muscles my sista flex.

My sista doesn mind smears of grease and dirt.
My sista'll reduce yu with sheer muscle hurt.
my sista says no guy goin keep her phone-bound –
with own car mi sista is a wheel-hound.

      I sey I wohn get a complex
      I wohn get a complex.
      Then I see the muscles my sista flex.

James

Self-Love

I love me very much,
I know I always shall;
I never find me boring;
I am my own best pal.

I'll never let me down
The way that others do;
I shall ignore all rivals;
I'll stick to me like glue.

When other people moan
That life gets worse and worse,
I gaze into the mirror
At Mr Universe

Who smiles and nods at me;
We both know what is meant:
'How could such faithful lovers
Fail to be content?'

And yet I must confess
At times I feel a touch
Perplexed that other people
Don't love me just as much.

And, when the lights go out
And looking-glasses wear
Cloaks of starless darkness,
However hard I stare

I see no answering gaze
And, cold as steel or stone,
Looms the bitter knowledge
That I am quite alone.

Vernon

Teacher Said . . .

You can use
> mumbled and muttered,
> groaned, grumbled and uttered,
> professed, droned or stuttered
> > . . . but *don't* use SAID!

You can use
> rant or recite,
> yell, yodel or snort,
> bellow, murmur or moan,
> you can grunt or just groan
> > . . . but *don't* use SAID!

You can
> hum, howl and hail,
> scream, screech, shriek, or bawl,
> squeak, snivel or squeal
> with a blood-curdling wail
> > . . . but *don't* use SAID!

> > . . . SAID my teacher.

Juanita

Vanya and the Kid

I am Vanya.
I sell hot dogs in Idaho Falls.
I serve my own mustard,
and it is *good* mustard,
good *Russian* mustard –
the kid eats it with bread.

The kid? Kurt
he calls himself in his funny accent
on the odd times he speaks.
He's gone now, South somewhere,
I don't know where. Took
off three weeks back.

You know him?
You say his name's Jurgen?
So, what's in a name?
He's a *good* kid, no trouble
to no one. Now he's gone.

Took with him
the monkey, rattlesnake and skunk
that shared his room
while he slept in the bath.
You looking for him?

If you find him bring him back.

Matthew

Give Yourself A Hug

Give yourself a hug
when you feel unloved

Give yourself a hug
when people put on airs
to make you feel a bug

Give yourself a hug
when everyone seems to give you
a cold-shoulder shrug

Give yourself a hug –
a big big hug

And keep on singing,
'Only one in a million like me
Only one in a million-billion-trillion-zillion
like me.'

Grace

Horace The Horrid

The day that baby Horace hatched
his proud mum gave a ROAR,
then stomped around to show him off
to her monster friends next door.
She named him HORACE THE HORRID –
she was sure he'd be quite a lad –
but soon it was clear, to her horror,
that Horace just wasn't bad.

You're supposed to EAT children, Horace,
not ask them out to play!
You're HORACE THE HORRID, Horace,
PLEASE put that teddy away!

Those feet are for kicking, Horace;
don't hide your claws under the mat!
That playpen's your BREAKFAST, Horace,
You're a MONSTER, remember that!

I'm sorry, said Horace, bowing his head.
I'm sorry to be such a bore,
but I'd rather eat carrots than children
and I really don't know how to roar.
And he carried on humming his quiet hum
till his mother grew quite wild,
but Horace the Horrid just opened his mouth
and smiled and smiled and smiled.
He opened his gummy, grinny mouth

    and smiled

        and smiled

            and smiled.

Judith

The Barkday Party

For my dog's birthday party
I dressed like a bear.
My friends came as lions
and tigers and wolves and monkeys.
At first, Runabout couldn't believe
the bear was really me. But
he became his old self again
when I fitted on his magician's top hat.
Runabout became the star, running about
jumping up on chairs and tables
barking at every question asked him.
Then, in their ordinary clothes,
my friend Brian and his dad arrived
with their boxer, Skip. And with us
knowing nothing about it, Brian's dad
mixed the dog's party meat and milk
with wine he brought. We started
singing. Runabout started to yelp.
All the other six dogs joined –
yelping:

Happy Barkday to you
  Happy Barkday to you
Happy Barkday Runabout
  Happy Barkday to you!

James

Sister

Tell me a story!
Lend me that book!
Please, let me come in your den.
I won't mess it up,
so *please* say I can.
When? When? When?

Lend me that engine,
that truck – and your glue.
I'll give half of my old bubblegum.
You know what Dad said
about learning to share.
Give it *now* –
or I'm telling Mum!

Oh, *please* lend your bike –
I'll be careful this time.
I'll keep out of the mud
and the snow.
I could borrow your hat –
the one you've just got . . .

                        said my sister.

and I said

NO!

Juanita

Mister Goodacre's Garden

The neighbours say he's weird and wicked
Just cause Mister Goodacre won't mow down
His high grass or thicket,
(Their own lawns look ready
for billiards or cricket)

I guess he just loves tall grass waving
I think the length of his dandelions amazing,
But the neighbours keep throwing him these
spearing-looks,
Which seem to say, 'You're lowering the tenor
Of the neighbourhood.'

Mister Goodacre just stands there
Whistling carefree,
Waving a water-gun for all to see;
'Think me lazy,' he says, 'think me crazy,
But I will defend my dandelions and daisies.'

More power to your wild flowers, Mister Goodacre,
But while you're basking . . .
I'm afraid the neighbours
Are planning a grass-murder
With their lawn-mowers.

Grace

Hair-Raiser

Why are there hairs in your nose, Daddy;
why all those hairs in your nose?
Those are vibrissae, my darling;
vibrissae, as everyone knows!

Why are their hairs on your chest, Daddy;
why are there no hairs on mine?
Hairs on your chest will come later, my son;
hairs on the chest take some time!

Why's there no hair on your head, Daddy;
why not a hair on your head?
Hair on the head is an optional extra –
now eat up your dinner, then *bed*!

Meals on Wheels

Bombing down the motorway
Doing ninety miles an hour
From a Chinese takeaway
Roared a dish of sweet-and-sour.

Going the other way went past
A slower meal on wheels, a platter
Carrying a simply vast
Quantity of cod in batter.

While down a quiet country lane,
Slow and gentle on two wheels
Cycling on in sun and rain
Rode a bowl of jellied eels.

Next purred the almost silent voice
Coming from a shining car
Made by Messrs. Rolls and Royce,
Full of Russian caviar.

And finally the great dray horse
Hauled on wheels of steel and wood
Triumphantly our favourite course:
Roast beef and veg and Yorkshire pud.

Vernon

Getting There

Call for a taxi Maxie,
Or phone for a mini-cab;
Don't worry about the meter,
I'll gladly pick up the tab.

Ignore the doorman Norman,
The cabbies are all on strike;
It's got to be Shanks's Pony,
Or getting on your bike.

Jump on the ferry Jerry,
It sails on the morning tide;
All day the bars will stay open
On the port (and the sherry) side.

Leap on your cycle Michael,
And zoom away fast, then display
The proper hand-signal for Norman,
Should you happen to meet on the way.

On to your scooter Pooter,
As pompous as pompous can be;
The tin-tacks we've spread out will puncture
Your tyres and your vanity.

Into your Morris Doris;
I wish I'd been given the chance
To join you; we'd park and together
Alight for a quick Morris dance.

Drive the jalopy Poppy;
It's ancient but none of us care
How bumpy and lengthy the journey
As long as we get safely there.

Vernon

Smile

Smile, go on, smile!
Anyone would think, to look at you,
that your cat was on the barbecue
or your best friend had died.
Go on, curve your mouth.
Take a look at that beggar,
or that one-legged bus conductor.
Where's *your* cross?
Smile, slap your thigh.
Hiccup, make a horse noise,
lollop through the house,
fizz up your coffee.
Take down your guitar
from its air-shelf and play
imaginary reggae
out through the open door.
And smile, remember, smile,
give those teeth some sun,
grin at everyone,
do it now, go on, SMILE!

Matthew

INDEX OF AUTHORS AND FIRST LINES

James Berry

Judith Nicholls

Grace Nichols

Vernon Scannell

Matthew Sweeney

ABOUT
THE
POETS

James Berry

I was born in Jamaica, in a village near the sea.

Our area had no school libraries and no supply of any books. But Bible stories were like poetry to me.

I craved to know and understand things. The world about me puzzled me. My head wanted to make stories and poems. I felt stories and poems would take me into different ideas and different places and different situations. And I liked how some Bible stories worked things out cleverly and wonderfully. And they pleased me and made me think and wonder. Yet, really, none of my own attempts to write a poem ever came out right.

We kept two horses, two mules, a donkey, a milking cow, some pigs, some goats, lots of chickens, two dogs and a cat. And from six years old I had my own jobs to help look after the animals.

I grew up and came to see how much I learnt about the ways of our animals. Their bad ways, their good ways, their tricks, and their similar ways, all make me smile. All give me pleasure. And the animals come into my stories and poems for young readers.

Living in the UK now for many years, I find nothing is better than being lost in my own world of a story or a poem.

Judith Nicholls

Judith started as a Lincolnshire 'yellow-belly' but now lives in a churchyard in Wiltshire . . . She can hear the church organ without getting out of bed!

She wrote her first poem, *Eeyore's Birthday*, when she was seven but didn't start writing books until a couple of centuries later. She has now written or compiled over 35 books and has poems in over 200 anthologies. She also visits schools – over 300 so far – to share poems and run poetry workshops with pupils and teachers.

Judith's books include *Magic Mirror/Midnight Forest*, *Dragonsfire, Storm's Eye, Otherworlds* and *Earthways, Earthwise*.

Grace Nichols

I was born and brought up in the South American country of Guyana with my five sisters, one brother, mother, father, grandmother and three cats. As a child I was a regular book-worm, often sneaking a torch into bed with me to finish off a book after my father had switched off lights for the night.

When I left high school at sixteen I worked as a pupil teacher for about three years, then as a telecommunications clerk, then as a reporter with one of our national newspapers. I enjoyed writing feature articles and short stories, and after a visit to the Guyana rainforest I was inspired to write my first poem, which was about one of our spectacular water-falls, Kaiteur.

In 1977 I moved to Britain and since then have published many books for children and adults. *Come on into my Tropical Garden; Give Yourself a Hug;* and *No Hickory No Dickory No Dock* are among some of my children's books. I live in Lewes, near Brighton, and love walking along the sea when it's very wild. Of course the sea here isn't as warm as back home and the beach isn't sandy, but sitting or lying back on the pebble beach still gives my head a nice clear peaceful feeling.

Vernon Scannell

Vernon Scannell is very old but he thinks he doesn't look his age. His friends agree. They think he looks much older but are too kind to say so.

He has been a soldier in World War II serving with the Gordon Highlanders in North Africa and later took part in the D-Day landings in Normandy. He has been a professional boxer and, for a short time, a teacher of English in a boys' Preparatory School.

He has a brown dog called Sally and lives in Yorkshire on a diet of Tetley's Bitter and liquorice allsorts.

Mathew Sweeney

Matthew Sweeney was born in the north-west of Ireland, right by the sea. It's no ordinary sea, it's the Atlantic. When you stand on the beach there and look out, you'll know the first land you'd come to is Iceland. Since 1973 he has lived in London, missing the sea.

He writes for children and for adults. *The Flying Spring Onion* and *Fatso in the Red Suit* are his two books of poems for children, and *The Snow Vulture* is a children's novel.

He likes cooking, reading (though he read more as a child), playing golf (though he was much better as a teenager), going to the cinema and collecting cacti. Together with a friend he invented a board game. It's easier to get books published.

Acknowledgements

The publishers would like to thank the following for permission to reprint the selections in this book:

Penguin Books for 'Date-Beggin Sweet World Them', 'Seeing Granny', 'Listn Big Broda Dread, Na!', extracts from 'Scribbled Notes Picked up by Owners and Rewritten because of bad grammar, bad spelling, bad writing' ('Puppy-Dog', 'Kitten-Cat') and 'The Barkday Party' from *When I Dance* © James Berry 1988 first published by Hamish Hamilton Children's Books 1988; 'Ritual Sundance', 'Retirement Poem' and 'Okay, Brown Girl, Okay' from *Playing a Dazzler* © 1996 James Berry first published by Hamish Hamilton Ltd 1996.

Judith Nicholls and Faber & Faber Ltd for 'Orang-Utan', 'Christmas Story', 'Mosquito', 'Pass the Pasta!' and 'Hair-Raiser' from *Dragonsfire* © Judith Nicholls 1990 first published by Faber and Faber Ltd 1990; 'Sister' and 'Storytime' from *Midnight Forest* © Judith Nicholls 1987 first published by Faber and Faber Ltd 1987; 'Teacher Said' and 'Lines' from *Magic Mirror* © Judith Nicholls 1985 first published by Faber and Faber Ltd 1985. Judith Nicholls and Oxford University Press for 'He Loves Me, He Loves Me Not' from *Storm's Eye* © Judith Nicholls 1994 first published by Oxford University Press 1994. 'Pssst!' © Judith Nicholls 1988. 'Count Your Toes!', 'Horace The Horrid' and 'Hairy Story' © Judith Nicholls 1996 reprinted by permission of Judith Nicholls.

Curtis Brown for 'Break Dance' from *Lazy Thoughts of a Lazy Woman* © Grace Nichols 1989 first published by Virago 1989; 'Don't Cry, Caterpillar', 'Baby-K Rap Rhyme', 'Ar-A-Rat' and 'My Parakeet' from *No Hickory No Dickory No Dock* © Grace Nichols 1991 first published by Viking 1991; 'Come on into my Tropical Garden', 'For Forest', 'My Cousin Melda', 'I Like to Stay Up' from *Come On Into My Tropical Garden* © Grace Nichols 1988 first published by A&C Black Ltd 1988; 'Morning', 'When My Friend Anita Runs', 'Mister Goodacre's Garden', 'Give Yourself A Hug' from *Give Yourself A Hug* © Grace Nichols 1994 first published by A & C Black Ltd 1994.

Vernon Scannell for 'My Dog', 'Jason's Trial' and 'Naughty Nursery Rhymes' © Vernon Scannell 1996; 'Jam Roll In Custody', 'Jelly-lover', 'Meals on Wheels', 'The Girl I Did Not Marry', 'The Fable of Aunty Mable', 'The Porcupie' and 'Special Today' from *The Clever Potato* © Vernon Scannell 1988 first published by Hutchinson Children's Books 1988; 'Grannie', 'Self-love', 'The Young and Hopeful Lover' from *Love Shouts and Whispers* © Vernon Scannell 1990 first published by Hutchinson Children's Books 1990; 'Stickers', 'Emergency Stop', 'Upper-deck Driver' and 'Getting There' from *On Your Cycle, Michael* © Vernon Scannell 1991 first published by The Bodley Head Children's Books 1991 under the title *Travelling Light*.

Faber and Faber Ltd for 'Cows on the Beach', 'All the Dogs', 'Into the Mixer' and 'The Burglar' from *The Flying Spring Onion* © Matthew Sweeney 1992 first published by Faber and Faber Ltd 1992; 'My Party', 'Vanya and the Kid', 'Bubblebus' and 'Smile' from *Fatso in the Red Suit* © Matthew Sweeney 1995 first published by Faber and Faber Ltd 1995.